Morning Comes to Appalachia

Louisa Emmons

Morning Comes to Appalachia

ISBN-13: 978-0692668115 (Hollow Tree Press)
ISBN-10: 069266811X

Hollow Tree Press
P.O. Box 322
Morganton, NC 28680

All inquiries should be addressed to the author through the publisher.

Printed in the United States of America

About the Author

Louisa Emmons has written several books about North Carolina history: *Tales from a Civil War Plantation: Creekside* is the story of the plantation built by Colonel Thomas George Walton in 1836. The book won the Robert Bruce Cooke Family History Book Award from the North Carolina Society of Historians in 2014. Another book by Emmons, *Civil War Voices from Western North Carolina: Letters from the Battlefield and the Home Front* won the Society's Willie Parker Peace History Book Award in 2015. Also by Emmons is *Glen Alpine Springs Hotel: A History of Burke County's Finest Accommodation*.

CONTENTS

INTRODUCTION

Appalachia is a culturally unique and geographically beautiful segment of the Eastern United States which extends roughly from southern New York to northern Mississippi, according to the Appalachian Regional Commission. Nearly one-third of the counties in North Carolina, specifically those located in the western region, belong to that area of Appalachia known as the Southern Highlands. The Southern Highlands are populated largely by the descendants of immigrants from England, Scotland, Wales, Ireland and Germany who intermingled with the original inhabitants of Appalachia, Native American tribes. Out of this mixture was born a people who reflect the character traits of their ancestors who were industrious, tenacious, clannish, loyal, honest, and fiercely independent.

The history of a people is always intimately tied to the land where they have loved, fought and dreamed. Western North Carolinians waged war to form a nation during the Revolution, fought to preserve a way of life during the Civil War, and continue the struggle to embrace the advance of progress while rejecting the exploitation of their land. Their culture is a reflection of this struggle. It is also the means by which they preserve the memory of their land and people over time.

The historical events of Appalachia included here involve war, exploitation, and infamy: the Battle of Kings Mountain, the erratic logging of mountain slopes, and the Trail of Tears. There are the tales of journeys, both real and mystical, such as the movement along the Great Wagon Road which tells the story of the Scots-Irish immigration to North Carolina, and the Cherokee creation story which explains the mystical origins of mountains, animals and men. Cultural events capture the happier moments of life in Appalachia: making molasses, eating the wild grape known as a "scuppernong", and searching woods and fields for the bee tree with its hidden treasure. There are remarkable moments of quiet serenity spent observing the landscape: the early mornings in Appalachia, the slash of autumn color in the western mountains, and the flight of a bird upward from a wintry mountain stream.

This book is a lyrical history of Appalachia in western North Carolina, chronologically arranged to reflect cultural and historic episodes from the first eruption of the Appalachian Mountain range to the recent return of the peregrine falcon to western North Carolina. Each event is a moment in time which represents conflict and ends with the resolution of that conflict. When I reflect on the toil and struggle which have helped to form Appalachia, from the fiery genesis of its primal origins to its present day battle with poverty, it is the rising of the peregrine falcon that, to me, personifies the spirit of the people of Appalachia and their triumph over adversity.

1. APPALACHIA: THE LAND EMERGES

Beneath the shallow sea we waited
    quietly, passively, straddling the equator.
But the earth is never still, and the massive plates that formed us
    grew restless, smashing and colliding against one another,
    some sinking down beneath the ocean floor and some rising above.
And the Appalachians were born from that violent coupling.

We are ancient.
Four hundred and eighty million years ago we were born,
    in the Ordovician Period
    when the building of mountains first commenced in North America.
Out of the watery mouth of darkness along the ocean floor,
    thrust up from the ocean bed, we rose.
Plate by plate, we were welded together, a geologic giant.
    And when the seas receded, we stood mighty.

The great land mass, Pangaea, began to break apart
    and the splintered land masses drifted across the earth
    two hundred and twenty million years ago.
The volcanic forces that formed us
    were stilled and we began slowly to weather and erode.
Once-jagged giants became gentle.
    By the end of the Mesozoic Era
Time and weather had eroded us almost to a flat plain.

But during the Cenozoic Era, we were violently uplifted once more,
    and streams formed which cut gashes deep into our bedrock
    and carved valleys and canyons across our topography.
The streams which coursed down our sides took rocks with them,
    carefully laying them down as they passed through the lowlands.
And the stones became soil, and the paths of streams moved and changed,
    opening new channels, abandoning old riverbeds,
    forming a smooth and bearded visage with stubble of pine and oak.

We are gentle now, with mountain laurel and worn rock faces
Concealing the lair of the red fox and the nest of the sleepy owl,
Reflecting in mountain pools the silvery slip of the moon.
Come and see. We are gentle now. But we are ancient and proud.

2. CHEROKEE CREATION STORY

In the time before the Dawn, all was water, and the water was everywhere
    For there was no land,
Only the stone arch that formed the bowl of the sky where the stars were born
    And the dark sweep of water moved.

The creatures dwelt in Galun'lati beyond the stone arch
    And no one knew who made them.
One of the creatures, Water Beetle, longed to know the depths of the dark sea,
    And he knew no fear of unknown things,
So Water Beetle dove down, down, down to the bottom of the great waters
    And brought up mud, so much mud
That it became land.
    But the land was not fit for creatures, and the First Man had not yet come.
The mud grew and grew until it became an island
    Fastened by slender chains to the bowl of the sky
Where it was bound fast and where it hung lightly on the swell of the sea.

The great birds of creation came down, one by one,
    Black Crow, Shy Quail and Sacred Eagle.
But they could not light upon the earth for it was too soft.
    The Great Buzzard, whose wings were mighty, flew low over the land,
And where the tips of his wings brushed the earth, deep valleys were carved.
    Where Buzzard's wings swept skyward majestic mountains thrust upward
Toward the dome of the sky.

And as the earth dried, the creatures descended one by one from Galun'lati
    And came to inhabit the valleys and the peaks and the rivers.
But the land was covered in darkness for Sun had not yet come
    And there was no warmth in the land.
And so the creatures drew down the Sun, but it was too close to the earth
    And it burned those who came too close to its scorching heat.
The shell of Crawfish was burned a brilliant red,
    So his meat was no longer fit to be eaten by Cherokee.

Cherokee was the First Man, and his spirit brother was Medicine Man
    Who knew the ways of the Great Spirit.
Medicine Man lifted his arms heavenward
    Until Sun rose seven times higher and rested beneath the stone bowl of the sky
Where it traveled along a path from East to West, day by day.

The Great Spirit hovered over the earth
   And commanded the plants and creatures
To be vigilant for seven days.
   Owl and Panther heard the voice of the Great Spirit and stayed awake,
   Though others did not,
And that is why Owl and Panther are creatures of the night
   Whose eyes see that which Man cannot.

Cedar, Holly, Pine, Spruce and Laurel, too,
   Heard the voice of the Great Spirit and remained wakeful.
That is why they bear vesture of noble green all year long
   While other trees mournfully shed their leaves.

The plants and the creatures of the earth heard the voice of the Great Spirit
   And hearkened to his word and his wisdom,
And because creation understood
   The earth is a good place for Cherokee.

3. THE GREAT WAGON ROAD
(SCOTS-IRISH IMMIGRATION, 1750-1780)

Down the Great Wagon Road from Pennsylvania we came,
>Lately landed in the New World.
Fresh from the linen factories of Ireland we came,
>Abandoning with sorrow our sheep farms,
Longing to practice our faith without fear,
>Escaping the oppression of high rent.
Desperate we came, some of us,
>And we indentured ourselves to those who would allow us to work,
For we were industrious people who longed to work
>And who were willing to work hard.
Through the Shenandoah Valley of Virginia we streamed,
>Pouring across the woods and fields,
Over the wagon traces and through the hollows,
>Past mountain coves and across rivers,
Down to the Southern Appalachians,
>Spreading across piedmont North Carolina in the 1750s.
You call these lands names like Yadkin and Polk, Rutherford and Wilkes,
>But when we felled great oaks and mighty chestnuts
>to frame our cabins and fences,
We honored these lands as our home.
>In the 1760s we journeyed across Burke and Yancey, Watauga and Davidson.
Soon, there was no piece of ground in North Carolina
>Upon which our restless feet had not trod,
And by the time of the American Revolution in 1776, we were proud colonists
>Known for our loyalty, our thrift, our honesty, our determination.
We became the backbone of the Overmountain Men
>Who drove the British from the Carolinas.
We fought with passion to be self-governing
>Because freedom had always been our rallying cry.
Sprung from the lowlands of Scotland,
>Dispersed to the rocky shingles of Ireland,
Across a fierce sea to America we came.
>And we knew no rest until we were free.
We are Americans. We are North Carolinians. We are Scots-Irish.

4. THE BATTLE OF KINGS MOUNTAIN (1780)

In the western wilderness where the fierce bear and the snarling catamount dwelt,
    We lived gaunt and strong,
Imperiled by the shadow of the Cherokee,
    Menaced by the turbulent river,
Men unafraid and unbroken.

From over the western ridge of the Appalachian Mountains we heard the cry.
    Beyond the far mountains from Gilbert Town
Where came the threat from Major Ferguson
    That he would lay waste our country with fire and sword.
We knew what we must do.
    We would cross over the mountains and defeat Ferguson.

Colonel Isaac Shelby and Colonel John Sevier sent out the call
    To rally us from the hills and valleys of North Carolina,
From the mountain settlements of southwestern Virginia and northeast Tennessee.
    Riders were dispatched to the north and to the east to rally the Patriots,
To the valleys of the Watauga, Nolichucky, and Holston River the word went out.
    General William Campbell called up the men of Virginia,
Mustered in Abingdon on the banks of Wolf Creek.

Colonel Benjamin Cleveland mustered North Carolina patriots
    From Wilkes and Surry Counties in the slumbering Yadkin Valley,
And Tennessee men were mustered by the rapids of the Watauga River
    In Sycamore Shoals, Tennessee.
Patriot Mary Patton presented us with 500 pounds of black powder from her mill.
    We readied ourselves. And we waited.

Day by day our numbers grew until we were a thousand men strong.
    While we waited, our women and children
Gathered the parched corn and beef jerky we would eat.
    We mended our clothes, we readied our guns.
We mined lead for the coming confrontation.
    We were militia, we were volunteers.
You don't need to raise an army to defend your own home.

A burning sermon rang out from Reverend Samuel Doak:
    "Oh God of battle," he prayed over us, "arise in Thy might.
Avenge the slaughter of Thy people...
    Help us as good soldiers to wield the Word of the Lord and Gideon!"

With his words burning in our hearts, we marched south from Sycamore Shoals
	And across the misty Blue Ridge Mountains.
On our first night out we stashed the Patton black powder
	In a dry cave called the "Shelving Rock" to shelter it from the rain.

We snaked down the mountain, following the Yellow Mountain Road,
	An ancient Indian path that wound through the mountains.
At Yellow Mountain Gap, we gathered in a snowy meadow and fell into formation.
	Two of our Tennessee men were missing, and we feared the worst.
They were not patriots, they were Tories,
	Slipped away to warn the British of our plan.
We hastened onward.
	We marched and rode to the foot of the mountain and stopped at Roaring
	Creek.
Two days later we ascended the Blue Ridge Mountains to Gillespie Gap.

The Catawba Valley lay before us with two paths descending the mountains.
	We split our forces and marched,
Some of us through Wofford's Fort and some of us through North Cove.
	Two days later we arrived at Quaker Meadows in Morganton.
The land once called Rowan was now called Burke.
	Things were changing. Our forces reunited.

We made camp at Quaker Meadows on McDowell lands.
	Campfires fashioned from split rail fence posts
Dotted the darkened margins of the meadow,
	Sparks exploding upward and showering back to the earth
To illumine our eager and hungry faces.
	We were brothers, now joined by more brothers
Who had trekked from Elk Creek to camp with us at Quaker Meadows.

Onward we rode toward Gilbert Town and then to Cowpens.
	We were joined by our brothers from South Carolina and Georgia.
One thousand eight hundred men strong we were,
	All frontiersmen, mountain men, militiamen, patriots.

Nine hundred of our best riflemen set out that evening from Cowpens.
	Bitter and stormy the night and the rain.
We bundled our long rifles in our sodden cloaks to keep them dry.
	Twenty-one miles on weary mounts we had ridden already,
Thirty-five more miles we would ride through the night to take Ferguson.
	Dirt roads ran rivulets of mud, and we slumped in our saddles peering through
The heavy mantle of the oppressive darkness.
	We would take neither food nor rest that night.

Across the Broad River our mounts plunged.

 Ferguson waited for us at the top of a rocky, tree-covered mountain
Called Little Kings Mountain.

 We approached quietly, unseen. We dismounted and tied our horses.
Swiftly we advanced on foot, circling the base of the mountain.

 We heard the shrill blast of Ferguson's silver whistle
As he alerted the Loyalists that we had arrived.

 Unprepared for us, Ferguson had not fortified his camp.

Up the mountain, forward we plunged, rifles clutched tightly,

 Giving Ferguson and his men Indian war cries contrived to terrorize them.
That is how we fought as we fired from behind trees and rocks,

 Not as the British fought, but like the frontiersmen we were.
Ferguson's men fired high, over our heads,

 Trying to gauge the right angle to bring us down, and failing miserably.
But they had fierce bayonets, and at Ferguson's order

 They charged down the mountain to attack us with deadly bayonets fixed.
We retreated when we saw them charge.

 But we reloaded and came back again, aiming our rifles steady and true,
Executing one Loyalist after another.

We were bear hunters, and squirrel hunters and rabbit hunters.

 We knew how to fire cleanly from the cover of the trees,
And Carolina was our land.

 We would defend our home and our families.
Three times we pushed forward

 Until we reached the top of Kings Mountain.
Ferguson knew he was ours,

 And when he rode out into the heart of the battle
Seeking to fight his way through the Patriots,

 We shot him out of the saddle.
I guess God had the last word, as always,

 Because Ferguson never left the mountain, just as he had sworn.
We buried him where he fell.

 The Loyalists surrendered, but some of us remembered past injustices
And continued firing into their line.

 Colonel Shelby took charge, and the fighting ceased.
We now had prisoners, and wounded men, and the slumbering dead.

The dead we buried in shallow graves,

 Abandoned the wounded on the field to the mercy of God.
Quickly we moved on for fear that Cornwallis might overtake us if we lingered.

 Unable to carry out more than we came with
We burned the wagons at the battleground,

 Cast off the specter of Kings Mountain.

Ferguson and his Loyalists we had devastated,
　　But we marched as angry men toward Gilbert Town
Remembering the threats and the disloyalty of our enemies
　　Who had given their allegiance to a foreign king.

At Aaron Biggerstaff's farm in Gilbert Town
　　We held a trial and found thirty men guilty of war crimes against us and our
　　kinsmen.
Pine knot torches lit the night as we hanged the traitors,
　　Three at a time we hanged them from the branches of an oak tree.
Nine Loyalists were hanged,
　　And we left them twisting from the limbs of the Gallows Oak
As a message to those who would betray the Patriots.
　　We gave our prisoners to Colonel Cleveland and Major Winston.

We turned toward home.
　　Mountain men.
Back we marched and rode, across the valleys and over the mountains,
　　Parting from our brothers with a nod
As if we had never met and just defeated a powerful enemy.
　　We were bound for hearth and home, ready to hunt,
Riding to reunite with our families,
　　Ready to see the thin column of smoke rising from our chimneys
Over the western ridge of the Appalachians.

5. THE BEE TREE

The sourwood her summer raiment wears
    Cloaked in summer fringe in leafy wooded groves.
Clouds of insects surge up in the heat from dusty roads at midday
    Where brown sparrows bathe
And the tassels of wild grasses ripple and sway
    Beyond the rim of the wooded thicket.

By a tangle of briar, I pause at the edge of the field
    And peer across a flaxen colored sea toward the shadowy grove.
I know where they live, the bees of summer.

I approach, curious, with drowsy calm,
    To behold the bees in streams vibrating on the languid air.
With golden, contented hum they ply their busy drift, curious and darting,
    And I follow them with caution,
Searching with my eyes the darkened hollows of the sourwood,
    Scanning shadowy passageways where the sun cannot filter.

I think I know where the honey lies hidden,
    Deep inside the sourwood.
Sticky sweet, dripping down, snug within a bee-made comb
    Waxen and fragrant with the pollen of wisterias and clover,
Redolent with the faint scent of honeysuckle and old wood.

Shall I disclose to the world
    A secret richer than a hidden sea,
A world within a world
    Where the bees of summer
    Dwell safe within the bee tree?

6. THE HIDDEN RIVER
(LINVILLE CAVERNS)

From beneath lichened rocks, cool and smooth along their edges,
    A hidden river flows precipitously,
Ghostly fish glide silver, suddenly,
    Upward from currents deep,
Escaped from a labyrinthine darkness
    Out of a cave of limestone
    Into the light of day.

Pioneers long ago traced the fish whose subterranean path
    Crossed buried rivers and coursed through dark and stone,
Concealed between rocky structures, following tunnels,
    Navigating the matrix of a stonework grid immovable
Where Cherokee once trod light-footed
    And Civil War deserters were sheltered
    From the revealing light of day.

Evermore, the hidden river runs, borne along a pathway
    Where indigenous life obscures its source.
It trembles then balances, delicate,
    At the feet of an immutable boundary
Where the wings of brown bats flit and come to rest
    Within the deep recesses incising shadowy walls
    Not pierced by the light of day.

7. THE TRAIL OF TEARS (1839)

We gave you corn, squash and potatoes when your people hungered,
     Our men taught you how to fish, hunt and farm our lands and waters.
With gnarled hands, our women taught you how to use native plants for medicine.
     We owned sawmills and general stores, we were blacksmiths and millers.
Your language we learned from your missionaries
     Though we were proud of our own language, created by Sequoyah.
The tribe was our society, and coexistence was the creed that sustained us.

But some wanted Cherokee land on which to plant their crops,
     To mine for the gold that had been discovered on our land,
To create plantations where our fathers lived and worked.
     So that others might prevail, all the laws of the Cherokee Nation
Were declared to be null and void.
     By one vote we lost the right to be a people existing in our own land.
We were driven from our native land and marched to Oklahoma.

We left behind the graves of our fathers,
     And the gentle hands of our grandmothers weaving.
We were forced to abandon the Oconaluftee River where we fished,
     The hollows and coves where we hunted for deer,
And the green hills where our children had played.
     The ghosts of the wind whispering through the hollows
And the hoot of the owl in lonely places were lost to us.

We were dragged from our homes, stripped of our belongings,
     Incarcerated in camps.
Food and water were scarce, disease was rampant.
     We were given wagons and horses for the journey,
     but only for the old and the sick.
The rest of us walked, hurried along through the snow barefooted.
     Four thousand out of fifteen thousand of our Cherokee people died
Between October 1838 and March 1839.
     Our journey of despair we called, "The Trail Where We Cried."

Over a thousand of our people hid in the coves and valleys from the soldiers.
     Among them was brave Tsali, who escaped with his family into the mountains.
We were told that if Tsali came forward, the others in hiding would be spared.
     So Tsali came, but he and his sons were executed
     Near the mouth of the Tuckasegee River.

11

A hundred years later, a dam was built
    And his grave was flooded by Fontana Lake.
The site of his sacrifice is forever lost to our children.
    The thousand who stayed behind became the core of our new tribe.
Like the mighty eagle, we have taken wing and surmounted our grief.
    We have swept away the darkness that once covered our land.
Our bitter tears have dried and the bones of our forefathers still slumber in the earth.
    From out of darkling waters, the ghosts of Tsali and his sons have risen.
Our spirit grandmothers weave their intricate baskets of willow and rivercane,
    Vessels which contain our dreams and the memories of our other life
    At a time when we walked along a trail not of our own choosing.

8. AUTUMN IN APPALACHIA

A crackle of hoar frost, delicate-patterned
    Follows the rise and fall of the field
Which we have long since abandoned
    For the fire on the hearth.
We are drawn close to the flames
    Scarlet and vermilion, lapped by blue flickers.
Our eyes mesmerized, we huddle near
    With cheeks burning.
But autumn lures us out again,
    Turning up our collars.
We feel the rough scratch of thick socks
    And the flapping fringe of woolen scarfs.
The gust of the wind is drawing us
    Down the slope, past the hickory trees in golden groves,
Throwing down their bitter harvest for the squirrels.
    Golden beech trees radiate their own light,
Illuminating the footpath where we pass.
    Across the valleys a flame sweeps,
Brighter and keener than a sword,
    Stirring and gladdening the wayward spirit of autumn.
Burning maples troop up the mountainside,
    Their russet banners fluttering.
The sourwood shakes her ruddy leaves,
    Her trembling white fringe lifting and imploring.
We gaze back up the mountain from hollows deep
    At fiery valleys that called us out in wonder at dawn.
At twilight, we turn our backs to the autumn wind,
    Seeking the tamer fire of our own hearth.

9. IN PRAISE OF THE WILD GRAPE

Hail to the impeccable wild grape,
    Beloved native fruit of the Old North State!
Call it a muscadine,
    Red and purple-black, in glossy loose clusters
With starry leaves and sweet fragrance
    Carried on the warm air of late summer and autumn,
Bursting, falling readily, heavily from a tendrilled vine.

Gold-bronze and dusty is the scuppernong,
    Child of the muscadine family,
Sweet and fruity, colossal and luscious
    With skin thick and bitter
Between the teeth.
    Juicy and seed-filled
Pale green pulp bursts through the skin
    Pleasant and mellow on the tongue.

She is the fruit of dreamers who recline in summer grasses
    By the lip of the Arcadian river,
Lulled to half-wakefulness in pastoral settings
    Drowsy and temperate at the edge of verdant fields.
Raise the goblet of gladness in praise of her delights,
    The libation of yearning for her tender fruitfulness,
The mellow, the noble, the sun-warmed wild grape!

10. MOUNTAIN MOLASSES

October arrives, crisp and clear, with autumnal skies and brilliant leaves.
　　It is time to make molasses.
We planted our sorghum seeds in May, deep in the red clay they love,
　　Faithfully fertilizing and weeding them, knowing the treasure they would bring.
And they have rewarded us richly!

We strip the leaves from the cane stalk as it stands tall in the field.
　　We cut off the dark brown seed pods with the knife at a slant
And haul the stalks to our cane mill.
　　Time was, we had mules that ran the cane mill,
　　but now we have motors to help us.
Times have changed, but not molasses!

The mill squeezes the cane juice out of the stalk
　　And we strain it through clean white cloths,
And then we wring the juice out of the cloths.
　　It's a lot of work with a lot of reward.
We pour the cane juice into big boiler pans.
　　My pans hold close to a hundred gallons of cane juice.
Then we light a fire under that juice, a slow, even, steady fire.

When the juice starts to boil, we skim it with a strainer constantly
　　From one end of the boiler to the other and back.
It takes six or seven hours of constant skimming to make molasses.
　　If you're going to make molasses, you'd better have a big family,
Because they will all take turns skimming and stirring.

Is it ready?
　　When you see it turn thick and yellow,
When large bubbles like frog eyes rise to the surface
　　The molasses is ready.
We strain it off into big pots and then pour it hot into mason jars.
　　Now, it is time to relish our reward!
Thick, rich and dark
　　We eat molasses with hot homemade biscuits and butter and strong coffee,
Lifting the cup to our lips, our steamy breath rising on the chill, crisp air.

11. JUDACULLA ROCK
(JACKSON COUNTY)

Tsul' Kalu, the Great Slant-Eyed Giant,
Was known to the Cherokee as a fierce hunter.
Tsul' Kalu summoned the rolling thunder and the stinging rain,
He snapped the backs of leaden boulders like the crack of a lightning bolt
And splintered tree trunks with a colossal fist.
The one who would guzzle the Tuckasegee River dry
And stride across the peaks of Balsam Mountain,
The one the Cherokee called Tsul' Kalu
We know as Judaculla.
His mighty boulder rests along the old Cherokee trail
East of Caney Fork Creek, immovable and immutable.
Judaculla's hunting laws were inscribed on that stone,
Ancient petroglyphs scratched by dagger-like nails,
And the images he depicted were primitive, mysterious:
Stick men, deer tracks, claw marks, wings, suns,
and the marks of flowing streams.
Some believe the sacred rock carvings depict the victory of native tribes
In ferocious battles long ago.
But who can say?
And who would contradict Judaculla?

12. LOGGING ON MT. MITCHELL
(MT. MITCHELL RAILROAD 1911-1914)

Our horses stamp impatiently, snorting out their smoky breath
    Into the brisk November air,
Shifting back and forth with eyes rolling as we back them up to the conveyance.
    The mules are dispassionate, standing, chewing the bit
As we strap them to the long-bed wagon,
    Harnesses creaking, buckles and straps binding them to their burden.

Soaring spruce trees, motionless guardians, quiver when the saws bite into them,
    Resisting the teeth that will soon crack them from their moorings
And send them crashing to the mountain floor in a flurry of dust and startled wings.
    The clamorous voices of men, strident on the air,
Surge outward into the chill morning
    Shattering the early silence.

The iron engine awaits, billowing out clouds of steam which soon condense
    And trickle down from smokestack to steam box to cylinders.
Lurching forward, building momentum, she clatters along the rickety rails
    Brilliant sparks ricocheting from her steel tracks,
Her wheels grinding and squealing along a course
    Now scorched and shorn of vegetation.

Man, beast and machine are the bringers of change to the mountain.
    At twilight, horses and mules permeated with warmth and sweat,
Their bodies exuding heat, eyes sunken with tiredness, heads carried low,
    Return to their chinked barns to bury their noses in dusty troughs of corn.
The iron engine, silent now in the roundhouse, stands stiff with iron grown cold.
    And man gazes out upon the shifting landscape, and recollects, and moves on.

13. MORNING COMES TO APPALACHIA

Morning comes to Appalachia,
    Gossamer as silken thread,
Fog lifting out of the hollows,
    Damp rising upward off the river.

Mist hangs over ploughed fields,
    Vaporous and ephemeral.
Dark earth furrows river bottoms
    Rich and fertile, seeds slumber.

Muskrat bustles along the bank,
    Scuttling through the brambles.
Startled heron wings beat skyward,
    Willows trailing trembling fronds.

Silent-surfaced stream unbroken,
    Deep currents disturbing,
Bubbles rise upward stirring
    Mud-submerged leaves.

Wind lifts beneath limbs
    Aflutter and trembling.
Hawk peers with ruffled feather,
    Meadow mice crouch uneasy.

Sun glimmers chinked rail fencing,
    Spider web threads glisten
And foot trod, stilled, in wonder watches.
    Morning comes to Appalachia.

14. THOSE WHO SLEEP
(RIVERSIDE CEMETERY, ASHEVILLE)

Those who sleep in eternal reverie, we remember,
    Tucked beneath stone angels and weeping willows.
Resting among the broken columns and the laurel wreaths of Riverside
    Undisturbed are the bones of our beloved soldiers, statesmen, authors, friends.

Thomas Wolfe, venerated author, lies sheltered by the wings of a stone angel,
    Contemplating forever the starry dome of the Appalachian night sky.
William Sidney Porter, honored writer, surveys from his place of eternal repose
    The flurry of sparrows among the shadowy cedars,
    their fluttering in dusty paths.
James Martin, Robert Vance, Thomas Clingman,
    Ride no more into battle
With banners wildly whipping and the snorting of horses plunging and rearing.
    Three generals now sleep in groves of knotted oaks
Whose slender branches intertwine in protective canopy
    Over their slumbering forms,
Their ensigns forever folded and their mounts hushed in the twilight.
    Zebulon Vance, beloved governor and statesman, his burden laid down,
Rests in dreamy memory among the cool green ferns and the starry moss.

Some who sleep came from far shores.
    George Masa came to catalog the peaks of the Appalachians,
To photograph the splendor of the Blue Ridge Parkway,
    To toil for the preservation of our western mountains.
He has come to rest among the leaning stones
    And the roots of oaks thrust upward
Though his spirit wanders unbound over the ridges of the southern highlands.

Eighteen German sailors, captured in the coastal waters of North Carolina,
    Prisoners of war confined at Hot Springs,
Transferred to the United States Army Hospital in Asheville,
    Died in the Great Epidemic between 1918 and 1919.
Their guns stand long-rusted, their helmets empty,
    Beneath the evergreens they dream with pensive, unseeing eyes,
While their spirits slip through ethereal meadows.

The Star of David marks graves crowned with trailing ivy,
    While nearby brothers sleep beneath the gentle shadow of the Cross.
Hope awaits a day that will come when all their eyes are opened once more
    And from the centuries of their repose they shall awaken to joy!
Rest in peace, fellow travelers.

15. THE CHILDREN OF APPALACHIA

We are the children of Appalachia,
   The sons and daughters of the Cherokee, the Scots-Irish, the English,
   the Germans.
Proud descendants of warriors and pioneers,
   We came into the world in the modern era,
But we carry the knowledge of a bygone world.

We have seen the mists of autumn rise ghostlike from the hollows,
   Filtering through the gnarly briar patches and swirling upward
   from the trunks of sourwoods,
Heard the eerie cry of the hoot owl in the lonely darkness from our solitary beds,
   And clambered through the icy mountain streams of early spring
   with labored breath.

Can you split rails? Can you make molasses? Can you find the bee tree?
   Can you bring your baby brother?
We can still do these things, some of us.
   We have a wealth of happy times, though we may not have money.

Remember that we have pride and history when you think of us.
   Do not come to save us from ourselves.
Come to learn of us,
   And you may take away things more valuable than you came with.

We are the children of Appalachia.

16. THE PEREGRINE RETURNS TO APPALACHIA

I have skirted the mountain cabin in the hollow,
    Fled upward from the icy stream in winter
Feathers ruffled to the dank smell of plowed earth,
    Past bottom land sharp with crackling hoar frost and crouching catamount.

A flutter of wind disturbs the ghost of the Nantahala coal fields,
    Its breath scuttling along the rough terrain of blackened earth,
Scattering dead leaves before the glimmer of coming light,
    Huddling uneasily at the base of sourwood trees
Then scrabbling upward toward the roost of the great horned owl.

The lair of the fox in open fields borders the abandoned logging camps
    of Mt. Mitchell.
    The voices of men once shouted over the crash and tremor of mighty oaks
And the breath of mules blew smoky on the frosty air
    Where vague mists now hover along the ground, spiraling slowly upward.
Furled fiddleheads thrust forth from the earth,
    Unwinding along the narrow fingers of mountain streams
Where the soft voices of Cherokee children once laughed and whispered.

Spirit soldiers in homespun gaze with unseeing eyes at distant peaks,
    Measuring with a sigh the length and breadth of memory,
Still trudging along the Overmountain Trail to meet a spectral foe,
    Forever hearing the rise and fall of worn boots
Marching along a pathway long gone
    Where goldenrod and purple ironweed now spring upward
    from dusty roadside ditches
And soft rabbits linger in patches of jumbled briar.

Life will not be held down. It returns.
    Past all memory, past all grief,
The warm pulse of the loamy earth still beats
    Fine and free.

Rise up I fly wings spread
    Beyond the far mountains I lift,
Scattering darkness before me like broken wind.
    Rise above, I cry! Rise above!
And I am borne upward
    Star-bound, sky free.
Clear as a bell morning breaks.